www.providencebooks.net

Publisher Contact

Email:contact@providencebooks.net

Social media: facebook.com/providencebooks

Acknowledgements

The team at Providence Books would like to thank our friends, family, suppliers and customers for making our vision of creating the highest-quality books a reality. Thanks for purchasing and enjoy the quotes!

This page is intentionally left blank

This page is intentionally left blank

A lot of music you might listen to is pretty vapid, it doesn't always deal with our deeper issues. These are the things I'm interested in now, particularly at my age.

Annie Lennox

Actually, I'm quite a domesticated person. I love the little things of home.

Annie Lennox

Although I have lived in London, I have never really considered London my home because it was always going to be a stopping-off point for me, and it has been too.

Annie Lennox

Anita Roddick was amazing. Her presence in a room was full of light, and everything she worked to achieve still resonates now.

Annie Lennox

As a creative person, you just put something out into the consciousness of the society you live in.

Annie Lennox

As a mother, you have that impulse to wish that no child should ever be hurt, or abused, or go hungry, or not have opportunities in life.

Annie Lennox

Ask yourself: Have you been kind today? Make kindness your daily modus operandi and change your world.

Annie Lennox

Charity is a fine thing if it's meeting a gap where needs must be met and there are no other resources. But in the long term we need to support people into helping themselves.

Annie Lennox

Churches, depending on their policy, can do fantastic work with people in the community.

Annie Lennox

Dying is easy, it's living that scares me to death.

Annie Lennox

Every artist has to make their own statements and they have to live with them.

Annie Lennox

Fame for fame's sake is toxic - some people want that, with no boundaries. It's unhealthy.

Annie Lennox

Fear paralyses you - fear of flying, fear of the future, fear of leaving a rubbish marriage, fear of public speaking, or whatever it is.

Annie Lennox

Feminism is a word that I identify with. The term has become synonymous with vitriolic man-hating but it needs to come back to a place where both men and women can embrace it. It is particularly important for women in developing countries.

Annie Lennox

For me, pointing and clicking my phone is absolutely fine. People say that isn't the art of photography but I don't agree.

Annie Lennox

HIV/AIDS has no boundaries.

Annie Lennox

Having children, they're not your property. They need to figure out their own views. I think my daughters have a pretty healthy self-awareness, but I can't speak on their behalf.

Annie Lennox

Humankind seems to have an enormous capacity for savagery, for brutality, for lack of empathy, for lack of compassion.

Annie Lennox

I also started writing songs because I had this burning activity in my heart and had to express myself.

Annie Lennox

I am a communicator; that seems to be my natural place. And I'll always be passionate about the world, because it's so bonkers.

Annie Lennox

I am fascinated by history and particularly the Victorian era.

Annie Lennox

I can't understand why the front pages of newspapers can cover bird flu and swine flu and everybody is up in arms about that and we still haven't really woken up to the fact that so many women in sub-Saharan Africa - 60 percent of people in - infected with HIV are women.

Annie Lennox

I didn't want to be perceived as a girly girl on stage.

Annie Lennox

I don't feel there are enough women artists out there who are saying anything of tremendous relevance.

Annie Lennox

I don't have any interest to go to Israel. I don't think I'd ever have a cause to go.

Annie Lennox

I don't have clear-cut positions. I get baffled by things. I have viewpoints. Sometimes they change.

Annie Lennox

I don't take myself as seriously as some people think, and I'd hate anyone to think I was preaching. That's the last thing I want.

Annie Lennox

I don't think feminism is about the exclusion of men but their inclusion... we must face and address those issues, especially to include younger men and boys.

Annie Lennox

I don't want to be owned by a corporation and obliged to make a certain type of album. I want to be free.

Annie Lennox

I enjoy multi-tasking, so I want to do a lot of different things. I want to keep all the plates spinning.

Annie Lennox

I have a calling in my soul, if you like, to try to make my life in some way worthwhile. What is the value of my existence?

Annie Lennox

I have a lot to be grateful for.

Annie Lennox

I have a reputation for being cold and aloof, but I'm so not that woman. I'm passionate. I love my girls, being with my girlfriends, getting involved with issues that affect other women and children who are suffering.

Annie Lennox

I have always been a very visual person and a keen observer.

Annie Lennox

I have always felt a little homeless. It's a strange thing.

Annie Lennox

I have different hats; I'm a mother, I'm a woman, I'm a human being, I'm an artist and hopefully I'm an advocate. All of those plates are things I spin all the time.

Annie Lennox

I haven't lived my life through my daughters. Some parents devote everything to their children, which must be so hard, and it's very beautiful. But I'm a working parent, so I've always kept my own life.

Annie Lennox

I like where I live here, in London.

Annie Lennox

I love to be individual, to step beyond gender.

Annie Lennox

I love to make music and stay grounded.

Annie Lennox

I mean, I'm 48 years old and I've been through a lot in my life - you know, loss, whether it be death, illness, separation. I mean, the failed expectations... We all have dreams.

Annie Lennox

I only want to make music because I have a passion for it.

Annie Lennox

I sang a lot as a little girl and entered competitions. I loved singing in choirs, but it was as I got older that I really found my voice.

Annie Lennox

I see myself as a traveller.

Annie Lennox

I think Scotland could take a stand in a wonderful way, ecologically and morally and ethically.

Annie Lennox

I think life on the road really suits very egotistical men. It's set up for kings.

Annie Lennox

I think music is the most phenomenal platform for intellectual thought.

Annie Lennox

I think my daughters have a pretty healthy self-awareness but I can't speak on their behalf.

Annie Lennox

I think people in Great Britain are a bit jaded sometimes.

Annie Lennox

I understand what it is for a woman to want to protect their children and give them the best they can.

Annie Lennox

I used to be obsessed about how I presented myself. I didn't want other people dressing me because I didn't want to be treated like a clothes horse.

Annie Lennox

I want people to start thinking about what it means to be HIV-positive and to ask questions about that.

Annie Lennox

I want people to understand me as a person with views, not just performing songs.

Annie Lennox

I want to branch out. I want to write. I write poetry. I want to see my children grow up well.

Annie Lennox

I was born in 1954. My parents were brought up in the war years, and life was hard.

Annie Lennox

I was brought up in a tenement house in a working district. We didn't even have a bathroom! We had a gaslight in the hallway and a black-and-white TV.

Annie Lennox

I was never much of a one to win prizes... and certainly never placed too much value on their acquisition.

Annie Lennox

I was perceiving myself as good as a man or equal to a man and as powerful and I wanted to look ambiguous because I thought that was a very interesting statement to make through the media. And it certainly did cause quite a few ripples and interest and shock waves.

Annie Lennox

I watch 'Mad Men,' I knit scarves, I cook and am very, very normal. Honestly.

Annie Lennox

I will go out of my way to avoid the shopping crowds and the extreme consumerism - I hate all that.

Annie Lennox

I would like to see the gay population get on board with feminism. It's a beautiful organisation and they've done so much. It seems to me a no-brainer.

Annie Lennox

I would say that although my music may be or may have been part of the cultural background fabric of the gay community, I consider myself an outsider who belongs everywhere and nowhere... Being a human being is what truly counts. That's where you'll find me.

Annie Lennox

I wouldn't say that I've mellowed. I'm less mellow, perhaps.

Annie Lennox

I'd rather support the issues I truly believe in than give my vote to parties that court votes at the time of the election. I like to think that my vote strengthens the green foundation stone.

Annie Lennox

I'm a female but I have a masculine side and I'm not going to negate that part of myself.

Annie Lennox

I'm appalled the word feminism has been denigrated to a place of almost ridicule and I very passionately believe the word needs to be revalued and reintroduced with power and understanding that this is a global picture.

Annie Lennox

I'm from a working-class background, and I've experienced that worry of not having a job next week because the unions are going on strike. I know that because I don't come from a wealthy background.

Annie Lennox

I'm from a working-class background, and I've experienced that worry of not having a job next week because the unions are going on strike.

Annie Lennox

I'm just an ordinary person.

Annie Lennox

I'm not a Christian, but I think the Christian message is a good one.

Annie Lennox

I'm not a saint. I'm not an angel. I'm a human being.

Annie Lennox

I'm not intensely private - I talk a great deal about my life and my work - I just don't play the game to excess.

Annie Lennox

I'm not particularly attention-seeking.

Annie Lennox

I'm not really keen on comebacks. Eurythmics was an incredible thing. When I look back on that work, I feel very satisfied with it.

Annie Lennox

I've always tried to keep my integrity and keep my autonomy.

Annie Lennox

I've had my share of dark days of the soul. I try not to focus on it too much so it doesn't get to me.

Annie Lennox

I've never been a social person. When I grew up, the other girls would all be combing their hair and exchanging lipstick, and I just couldn't do that group thing.

Annie Lennox

I've never experienced chronic poverty, but I know what it's like to live on £3 a week.

Annie Lennox

I've thought about what is an alternative word to feminism. There isn't one. It's a perfectly good word. And it can't be changed.

Annie Lennox

If I hadn't been a singer, I might have been a photographer or an artist. But it's singing I love. I sing all the time, and I feel really good that I've expressed myself.

Annie Lennox

If people like your music, you can't guarantee they're going to love you.

Annie Lennox

If someone says something unpleasant, I can't say it doesn't smart a bit. It always does. Someone can take a really nasty swipe if they want because it kind of feels powerful for a person to write in a paper and get that thing out there.

Annie Lennox

If we value what we've inherited for free - from other women - surely it's right morally and ethically for us to wake up and say, 'I'm a feminist. '

Annie Lennox

If you want to open a supermarket chain and put your face all around the globe, selling your baby and your dog, if it makes you happy, who am I to disagree, as the song goes. But it's not for me. I've always tried to keep my integrity and keep my autonomy.

Annie Lennox

In a sense, the music business and I haven't always been the best of bedfellows. Artists often have to fight their corner. Your music goes through these filters of record labels and media, and you're hoping you'll find someone who'll help you get your work into the world.

Annie Lennox

It's a very telling thing when you have children. You have to be there for them, you've got to set an example, when you're not sure what your example is, and anyway the world is changing so fast you don't know what is appropriate anymore.

Annie Lennox

It's hard to tell how far women's individuality has come in the past twenty years.

Annie Lennox

It's not fair to compare one artist to another because they all come with their own sort of elements to the picnic, you know.

Annie Lennox

Life expectancy in many parts of Africa can be something around the age of thirty five to thirty eight. I mean you're very fortunate if you live to that age. In fact when I went to Uganda for the first time one of the things that occurred to me was that I saw very few elderly people.

Annie Lennox

Life is not quantifiable in terms of age, but I suppose in my fifties I am more grounded and more at ease in my own skin than when I was younger. I have a confidence that I didn't have before from the experiences I've had.

Annie Lennox

Making a Christmas album is looked upon by some people as the thing you do when you are heading towards retirement.

Annie Lennox

Men need to understand, and women too, what feminism is really about.

Annie Lennox

Money is a good thing and it's obviously useful, but to work only for money or fame would never interest me.

Annie Lennox

Most women are dissatisfied with their appearance - it's the stuff that fuels the beauty and fashion industries.

Annie Lennox

Motherhood was the great equaliser for me; I started to identify with everybody.

Annie Lennox

Motherhood was the great equaliser for me; I started to identify with everybody... as a mother, you have that impulse to wish that no child should ever be hurt, or abused, or go hungry, or not have opportunities in life.

Annie Lennox

Music is a great vehicle for communications, and I have a certain platform. I have an opportunity and I have to take it.

Annie Lennox

Music is an extraordinary vehicle for expressing emotion - very powerful emotions. That's what draws millions of people towards it. And, um, I found myself always going for these darker places and - people identify with that.

Annie Lennox

My issue with the state of women became incredibly stimulated when I was visiting developing countries and it became obvious that women bore the brunt of so many things in society.

Annie Lennox

Nelson Mandela is awe inspiring - a person who really sacrificed for what he believed in. I feel truly humbled by him.

Annie Lennox

One wouldn't want to have the same dilemmas at 50 as one had at 15. And indeed I don't. I have a very different take on life.

Annie Lennox

Our ancestors are totally essential to our every waking moment, although most of us don't even have the faintest idea about their lives, their trials, their hardships or challenges.

Annie Lennox

Over the years, I was never really driven to become a solo artist, but I was curious to find out who I was as an individual creative person. It's taken some time, but now I feel I've truly paid my dues. I guess I'm at a point now where I'm more comfortable in my own skin.

Annie Lennox

People ask me so many questions.

Annie Lennox

Please don't ask me for the actual answer to anything, because I don't have it. Because all I do is look at stuff and ask questions. What can I say? I just think the world's barking mad. Look, I'm not an expert. I'm just an ordinary person.

Annie Lennox

Pop stars are so busy having a career that they don't really have a lot of time for activism.

Annie Lennox

The dynamic between two individuals starts off with everything warm and nice and fabulous and good. Working and living together can serve you quite well, but when it starts to go wrong - oh, boy!

Annie Lennox

The future hasn't happened yet and the past is gone. So I think the only moment we have is right here and now, and I try to make the best of those moments, the moments that I'm in.

Annie Lennox

The general population still thinks HIV is something that came in the 80s and went away, or that it only affects the gay population or intravenous drug users.

Annie Lennox

The inner world is very potent for me - I don't ascribe to any God or Jesus or Buddha - I just have a sense of it and revere it along with the natural world and human consciousness.

Annie Lennox

The person who inspired me the most was a friend of mine, Anita Roddick. I know that Anita wasn't known to be an ardent feminist, but she truly was.

Annie Lennox

The word feminism needs to be taken back. It needs to be reclaimed in a way that is inclusive of men.

Annie Lennox

The world is a heartbreaking place, without any question.

Annie Lennox

There are two kinds of artists left: those who endorse Pepsi and those who simply won't.

Annie Lennox

There is a big difference between what I do onstage and what I do in my private life. I don't put my living room on magazine pages.

Annie Lennox

There's a lot of women's organisations, but they're all working separately. If you get people together, as a collaborative voice, it's strong.

Annie Lennox

Those in the developing world have so few rights - we take a lot for granted in the developed world.

Annie Lennox

We all fight over what the label 'feminism' means but for me it's about empowerment. It's not about being more powerful than men - it's about having equal rights with protection, support, justice. It's about very basic things. It's not a badge like a fashion item.

Annie Lennox

Whatever you do, you do out of a passion.

Annie Lennox

When I look at the majority of my own songs they really came from my own sense of personal confusion or need to express some pain or beauty - they were coming from a universal and personal place.

Annie Lennox

When you get to be nearly 60, you do take stock. You don't know what's around the corner.

Annie Lennox

When you go to Africa, and you see children, they're usually barefoot, dirty and in rags, and they'd love to go to school.

Annie Lennox

When you're that successful, things have a momentum, and at a certain point you can't really tell whether you have created the momentum or it's creating you.

Annie Lennox

Why are we not valuing the word 'feminism' when there is so much work to be done in terms of empowerment and emancipation of women everywhere?

Annie Lennox

Women's issues have always been a part of my life. My goal is to bring the word 'feminism' back into the zeitgeist and reframe it.

Annie Lennox

Women's issues have always been a part of my life.

Annie Lennox

You have to face things, have faith in what you do and go for it. Think, 'What's the worst that could happen?'

Annie Lennox

You just decide what your values are in life and what you are going to do, and then you feel like you count, and that makes life worth living. It makes my life meaningful.

Annie Lennox

You know, I would say that songwriting is something about the expression of the heart, the intellect and the soul.

Annie Lennox

You wouldn't find a Joni Mitchell on 'X Factor;' that's not the place. 'X Factor' is a specific thing for people that want to go through that process - it's a factory, you know, and it's owned and stitched-up by puppet masters.

Annie Lennox

This page is intentionally left blank

This page is intentionally left blank

This page is intentionally left blank

This page is intentionally left blank

This page is intentionally left blank